Beneath the Burrow

Beneath the Burrow

Matthew Petchinsky

B eneath the Burrow: Lessons from the Groundhog
	By: Matthew Petchinsky

Introduction: Insights into the Symbolic Life of the Groundhog

The groundhog, a humble yet fascinating creature, holds a place of profound significance in the cultural and symbolic tapestry of human history. Known for its role as a seasonal soothsayer in modern traditions like Groundhog Day, the groundhog's symbolic life extends far beyond its weather-predicting fame. Beneath the surface of its seemingly simple existence lies a rich narrative of resilience, introspection, and the cyclical nature of life.

A Seasonal Oracle

Every February 2nd, the groundhog emerges from its burrow to play the role of nature's oracle. This ritualistic event, rooted in ancient traditions, marks the intersection of folklore and natural observation. Historically, Groundhog Day evolved from the ancient celebration of Imbolc, a Celtic festival marking the midway point between the winter solstice and the spring equinox. The day symbolized the hope of renewal, light, and the return of life to the frozen earth. The groundhog, with its emergence, became a tangible symbol of this hope, representing humanity's desire to predict and control the uncontrollable forces of nature.

A Symbol of Cycles and Duality

The groundhog's life mirrors the cycles of nature, embodying the duality of retreat and emergence, dormancy and awakening. Through its annual hibernation and resurfacing, the groundhog reflects the rhythms of the earth itself—the ebb and flow of seasons, the death and rebirth inherent in nature. In its winter sleep, the groundhog becomes a symbol of introspection, encouraging us to reflect on our inner worlds and recharge. When it awakens, it symbolizes renewal and the courage to face the challenges of the coming year.

The Burrow: A Portal Between Worlds

The groundhog's burrow is not merely a shelter; it is a symbolic portal between two worlds. Above ground lies the visible, active world of light, growth, and vitality, while below ground exists the hidden, shadowy realm of rest, mystery, and regeneration. In myth and folklore, this duality often represents the balance between conscious and unconscious, life and death, or the known and the unknown. The burrow reminds us of the importance of both retreat and action, teaching us to find harmony between the visible demands of life and the unseen processes of personal growth.

Cultural and Mythological Significance

The groundhog, or woodchuck as it is also known, holds various meanings across cultures. In Native American traditions, it is often seen as a symbol of diligent preparation and foresight. The groundhog's industrious digging represents the hard work necessary to build a strong foundation, both physically and metaphorically. Its hibernation patterns align with themes of endurance and the wisdom to conserve energy for future challenges.

European settlers in North America brought their own traditions, merging Old World customs with New World observations. The groundhog replaced the European hedgehog as the weather predictor, a shift that underscores humanity's enduring connection to animals as guides and symbols.

A Mirror for Humanity

In many ways, the groundhog serves as a mirror for human experiences. Its careful preparation for winter resonates with our instinct to plan and prepare for uncertain futures. Its retreat into the burrow mirrors our need to withdraw and reflect during times of difficulty or transformation. Its cautious emergence into the world, testing the waters of safety and opportunity, reflects our own tentative steps into new endeavors.

The groundhog reminds us that life is a balance of activity and rest, action and contemplation, light and shadow. It invites us to embrace our own cycles of growth, to honor our need for both solitude and connection, and to find meaning in the rhythms of our lives.

The Groundhog as a Teacher

As we delve deeper into the symbolic life of the groundhog, it becomes clear that this creature offers profound lessons for those willing to look beyond its furry exterior. Its annual ritual, grounded in instinct and nature's rhythms, teaches us to attune ourselves to the cycles of the earth. It calls on us to recognize the value of both stillness and action, urging us to align our lives with the ebb and flow of time.

The groundhog's journey—its retreat, hibernation, and emergence—becomes a metaphor for our own journeys. Whether we face the harshness of winter or the promise of spring, the groundhog's story reminds us that transformation is always possible, and that within every ending lies the seed of a new beginning.

As we explore the chapters ahead, let us view the groundhog not just as a herald of weather, but as a guide to understanding the deeper rhythms of life. Through its humble existence, this unassuming creature offers insights into resilience, reflection, and renewal, inspiring us to navigate our own paths with wisdom and grace.

Chapter 1: The Groundhog's Journey Underground

The groundhog, often overlooked in the vast pantheon of symbolic creatures, leads a life of surprising complexity beneath the soil. Its journey underground is far more than a physical retreat; it is a metaphor for introspection, survival, and the enduring cycles of life. In this chapter, we explore the intricate details of the groundhog's subterranean existence, delving into the ecological, symbolic, and spiritual implications of its underground life.

An Architect of the Earth

At first glance, the groundhog's burrow may appear to be a simple hole in the ground, but upon closer inspection, it reveals an intricate and expertly designed structure. Groundhogs, also known as woodchucks, are meticulous architects, crafting burrows that serve multiple purposes, from shelter to storage.

A typical burrow consists of multiple chambers connected by a network of tunnels. Each chamber has a distinct purpose:

- **The Nesting Chamber**: Softly lined with grass and leaves, this area provides a safe, warm space for the groundhog to rest and rear its young.
- **The Storage Chamber**: Here, the groundhog may stockpile food to sustain itself during active seasons.
- **The Waste Chamber**: A unique feature of the burrow, this chamber is dedicated to waste, ensuring the living quarters remain clean and hygienic.

Burrows also feature multiple entrances and exits, designed to allow the groundhog to evade predators. These secondary openings are often hidden among vegetation, providing a vital escape route in moments of danger.

The Cycle of Hibernation

One of the most fascinating aspects of the groundhog's underground journey is its hibernation—a biological marvel that demonstrates the animal's adaptability and resilience. During the cold months of winter, the groundhog retreats to its burrow and enters a state of torpor, characterized by significantly reduced metabolic activity.

- **Physiological Changes**: The groundhog's heart rate drops from approximately 80 beats per minute to as low as 5 beats per minute. Its body temperature falls dramatically, conserving energy as food becomes scarce.
- **Survival Mechanism**: This period of dormancy allows the groundhog to endure the harsh conditions of winter without expending unnecessary energy. By living off stored body fat, it ensures survival until spring's abundance returns.

Hibernation is not merely a survival tactic; it is a profound example of the cyclical nature of life. Just as the groundhog conserves its energy during winter to thrive in spring, we, too, can learn to honor periods of rest and renewal as essential parts of our personal journeys.

The Burrow as a Symbolic Haven

Beyond its practical function, the groundhog's burrow holds deep symbolic significance. It represents a sanctuary, a place where the groundhog can retreat from the dangers and demands of the outside world. In mythology and folklore, such hidden spaces are often associated with introspection, transformation, and rebirth.

- **A Place of Safety**: The burrow's concealed entrances and labyrinthine tunnels mirror the human need for privacy and protection in times of vulnerability.
- **A Womb of Renewal**: The underground chambers, where life slows down to a near standstill during hibernation, symbolize the womb—both a place of safety and a precursor to new beginnings.
- **The Threshold Between Worlds**: In many cultures, burrows and underground spaces are seen as thresholds between the conscious and subconscious, the living and the spiritual. The groundhog's journey underground can be viewed as a metaphor for delving into one's inner self to uncover hidden truths and insights.

Ecological Contributions of the Burrow

The groundhog's burrow is not just a home; it is a vital component of its ecosystem. These structures, often extending over 20 feet in length and reaching depths of up to 6 feet, serve as habitats for other animals, including rabbits, skunks, and foxes, once the groundhog abandons them.

- **Soil Aeration**: The digging process helps to aerate the soil, promoting better water penetration and nutrient cycling. This natural tilling benefits plant growth and contributes to the health of the ecosystem.
- **Biodiversity**: By creating safe havens for other species, groundhog burrows enhance local biodiversity, ensuring a balanced and thriving ecosystem.

Through its underground activities, the groundhog demonstrates the interconnectedness of life. Its efforts not only sustain its own survival but also contribute to the well-being of its environment, reminding us of our own responsibility to nurture and protect the world around us.

Lessons from the Groundhog's Subterranean World

The groundhog's journey underground offers profound lessons for us as individuals. Its life beneath the soil teaches us the value of preparation, resilience, and introspection. Just as the groundhog retreats to its burrow to weather the harshness of winter, we, too, can create safe spaces—both physical and emotional—where we can reflect, recharge, and prepare for life's challenges.

- **Preparation**: The groundhog's careful construction of its burrow and its meticulous accumulation of fat reserves highlight the importance of planning for the future.
- **Adaptation**: Hibernation serves as a reminder that slowing down and conserving energy during difficult times can be a powerful strategy for survival and growth.
- **Introspection**: The symbolic act of going underground encourages us to look inward, examining our lives and uncovering hidden strengths and opportunities.

Emerging from the Depths

As winter fades and the promise of spring looms, the groundhog emerges from its burrow, bringing with it the wisdom of its underground journey. This transition from darkness to light, from dormancy to activity, is a powerful symbol of renewal and hope. It reminds us that even in the most challenging times, there is always the potential for growth and new beginnings.

The groundhog's journey underground is a story of resilience, connection, and transformation. It is a narrative that inspires us to embrace the cycles of our own lives, to honor the moments of retreat as much as those of action, and to find strength and meaning in the depths of our own existence. As we continue to explore the groundhog's life in this book, let us carry these lessons with us, finding inspiration in the quiet, unassuming wisdom of this remarkable creature.

Chapter 2: Lessons from Nature's Calendar

Nature operates on a rhythm as old as time, a calendar that governs the cycles of life, death, and rebirth across all living things. Among its many timekeepers, the groundhog serves as a unique figure in understanding these rhythms. Its behavior, dictated by instinct and environment, provides profound insights into the interconnectedness of natural cycles and human life. In this chapter, we delve into the lessons offered by nature's calendar through the lens of the groundhog's seasonal patterns and explore how these lessons can shape our understanding of time, change, and resilience.

The Groundhog as a Seasonal Barometer

Groundhogs are intimately attuned to the seasonal changes that govern their survival. Every aspect of their behavior—from hibernation to foraging—is aligned with nature's calendar. By observing these behaviors, we gain a deeper understanding of how living beings can thrive by synchronizing their lives with natural rhythms.

- **Spring Emergence**: The groundhog emerges from its burrow in early spring, signaling the arrival of longer days and warmer weather. This event, often celebrated on Groundhog Day, symbolizes hope and the anticipation of renewal.
- **Summer Abundance**: During the summer months, the groundhog forages extensively, building up fat reserves to sustain itself during the coming winter. This period of activity highlights the importance of preparation during times of plenty.
- **Autumn Preparation**: As the days shorten and temperatures drop, the groundhog's behavior shifts toward conserving energy. It becomes more focused on final preparations for hibernation, reminding us of the need to adapt as circumstances change.
- **Winter Rest**: In winter, the groundhog retreats into its burrow to hibernate. This phase of dormancy underscores the necessity of rest and regeneration as part of life's cycle.

These seasonal behaviors illustrate the importance of living in harmony with the natural world. By understanding and respecting these cycles, humans, too, can find balance and resilience in the face of change.

Lessons in Patience and Timing

The groundhog teaches us the value of patience and timing, qualities often overlooked in the fast-paced modern world. Nature's calendar operates without haste, unfolding with precision and purpose. The groundhog's instinctive understanding of when to act and when to rest offers a model for finding equilibrium in our own lives.

- **Patience in Rest**: The groundhog's hibernation is a testament to the power of patience. By conserving energy during winter, it ensures its survival until spring. This lesson reminds us that periods of stillness are not wasted time but essential for future growth.
- **Timing of Action**: The groundhog emerges from its burrow only when conditions are favorable, demonstrating the importance of timing in decision-making. Acting too soon or too late can have dire consequences, both for the groundhog and for us.

Incorporating these principles into our lives can help us navigate challenges with greater wisdom, ensuring that our efforts are well-timed and effective.

The Cyclical Nature of Life

At the heart of nature's calendar is the concept of cycles—patterns that repeat and evolve, guiding all living things through the stages of existence. The groundhog's life is a microcosm of these cycles, offering valuable insights into the universal truths that govern life.

- **Birth and Renewal**: Each spring, the groundhog emerges to a world teeming with life. This season represents new beginnings and the endless potential for growth.
- **Maturity and Preparation**: Summer and autumn are times of activity and preparation, reflecting the importance of building a strong foundation for the future.
- **Death and Rest**: Winter brings a period of dormancy, mirroring the inevitability of endings and the necessity of rest before renewal.

By observing these cycles, we can learn to embrace change as a natural and necessary part of life. Just as the groundhog adapts to the seasons, we, too, can find strength and stability in the face of life's transitions.

Synchronizing Human Lives with Nature

In today's world, many people feel disconnected from the natural rhythms that once guided human life. The groundhog's adherence to nature's calendar serves as a reminder of the benefits of living in harmony with these cycles. By aligning our actions with the rhythms of the earth, we can enhance our well-being and resilience.

- **Seasonal Living**: Incorporating seasonal practices into our lives—such as eating locally grown foods, adjusting work and rest schedules, and engaging in seasonal rituals—can help us feel more connected to the natural world.
- **Mindful Observation**: Paying attention to the changes in our environment, as the groundhog does, can deepen our awareness of the world around us and foster a sense of gratitude for its beauty and complexity.
- **Adaptability**: Like the groundhog, we must learn to adapt to changing circumstances, recognizing that each season of life brings its own challenges and opportunities.

Symbolism of the Groundhog in Nature's Calendar

Beyond its biological role, the groundhog holds symbolic meaning as a keeper of nature's calendar. Its behaviors are rich with metaphor, offering insights into how we can navigate the complexities of time and change.

- **Emergence as Renewal**: The groundhog's spring emergence symbolizes the courage to face new challenges and the optimism that accompanies new beginnings.
- **Preparation as Wisdom**: The groundhog's diligent preparation for winter reflects the importance of foresight and planning in achieving long-term success.
- **Hibernation as Reflection**: The groundhog's winter rest serves as a metaphor for introspection and the power of stepping back to recharge and gain perspective.

Practical Applications of Nature's Lessons

The lessons of nature's calendar, as embodied by the groundhog, can be applied in countless ways to enrich our lives. Whether we are seeking personal growth, professional success, or greater harmony with the world around us, these principles offer a roadmap for navigating life's challenges and opportunities.

- **Setting Intentions with the Seasons**: Just as the groundhog's actions align with the changing seasons, we can use the natural calendar to set goals and intentions. Spring can be a time for new projects, summer for growth, autumn for reflection, and winter for rest.
- **Cultivating Resilience**: By understanding that life's difficulties are temporary and part of a larger cycle, we can develop the resilience to endure challenges and emerge stronger.
- **Finding Balance**: Nature's calendar reminds us of the importance of balance—between work and rest, action and reflection, and preparation and spontaneity.

The Eternal Wisdom of Nature's Clock

As we reflect on the groundhog's role in nature's calendar, we are reminded of the profound wisdom embedded in the natural world. The cycles of the seasons, mirrored in the groundhog's life, teach us that time is not a linear progression but a series of interconnected rhythms. By embracing these rhythms, we can live more fulfilling, harmonious lives.

The groundhog's journey through the seasons is a testament to the enduring power of nature's calendar. It invites us to step back from the rush of modern life and reconnect with the timeless patterns that sustain us all. As we continue our exploration of the groundhog's symbolic life, let us carry these lessons with us, finding inspiration in the cycles of renewal, growth, and transformation that define the natural world.

Chapter 3: Burrowing as a Metaphor for Reflection

In the natural world, the act of burrowing is an instinctive behavior for survival, safety, and sustenance. For the groundhog, burrowing is not only a practical necessity but also a symbol of its intricate relationship with the environment. When viewed through a metaphorical lens, burrowing becomes a powerful representation of human introspection, self-discovery, and the need to retreat inward to find clarity and renewal. This chapter explores the groundhog's burrowing habits as a rich metaphor for reflection, delving into its symbolic, psychological, and practical implications.

The Groundhog's Burrow: A Safe Haven

The groundhog's burrow is an engineering marvel—a complex system of tunnels and chambers that provide shelter and security. For humans, the metaphorical "burrow" is any space we create to find peace and respite from the chaos of the external world. It is in these personal havens that reflection and introspection flourish.

- **Physical Safety**: For the groundhog, the burrow offers protection from predators and harsh weather. For us, moments of retreat—whether in a quiet room, a meditative practice, or a reflective walk in nature—create a mental and emotional safe space.
- **Emotional Shelter**: Just as the burrow shields the groundhog, our metaphorical burrows shield us from life's external pressures, allowing us to pause and process our thoughts and emotions without distraction.

By understanding the purpose and structure of the groundhog's burrow, we can learn to build our own safe spaces for reflection and personal growth.

The Act of Digging: Unearthing Hidden Truths

The groundhog's burrowing is an act of transformation, reshaping the earth to create a sanctuary. Metaphorically, this process mirrors the human journey of self-exploration, where digging into one's subconscious can unearth hidden truths and bring clarity.

- **Breaking Ground**: The first steps of digging represent the courage to confront challenges and initiate self-exploration. It requires effort and persistence, just as introspection demands a willingness to face uncomfortable truths.
- **Reaching Depths**: As the groundhog tunnels deeper, it carves out a space for safety and rest. Similarly, delving deep into our thoughts and emotions allows us to find insight, healing, and understanding.
- **Shaping the Path**: The groundhog's burrow is intentionally designed, with distinct chambers for different purposes. This organization reflects the human ability to compartmentalize and process various aspects of our lives, organizing our thoughts to gain a clearer perspective.

The act of digging serves as a reminder that self-reflection is not always easy or immediate, but the rewards of discovering one's inner self are profound.

Burrowing and the Cycle of Renewal

Burrowing is not a one-time act; it is a continuous process tied to the cycles of nature. For the groundhog, burrows are revisited, expanded, or abandoned as seasons change. This cyclical nature reflects the ongoing human need for reflection and renewal.

- **Seasonal Reflection**: Just as the groundhog retreats to its burrow during winter, we often find ourselves turning inward during challenging times. These periods of introspection prepare us for eventual growth and action.
- **Emerging with Purpose**: After spending time underground, the groundhog emerges stronger and more prepared. Similarly, moments of deep reflection enable us to re-enter the world with renewed focus and purpose.
- **Adapting to Change**: The groundhog modifies its burrow as needed, demonstrating adaptability. In our lives, the spaces and methods we use for reflection may evolve over time, reflecting our changing needs and circumstances.

The metaphor of burrowing reminds us that self-reflection is a dynamic process, essential for adapting to life's ever-changing landscape.

Psychological Dimensions of Burrowing

From a psychological perspective, the act of burrowing can be seen as a metaphor for the inward journey of the mind—a process that helps us navigate emotions, memories, and personal challenges. The burrow becomes a symbol of the subconscious, a place where we store both fears and treasures.

- **Confronting Shadows**: The dark, hidden nature of the burrow represents the shadow self—the parts of our psyche that we often avoid. By entering our metaphorical burrows, we have the opportunity to confront and integrate these aspects, fostering personal growth.
- **Cultivating Self-Awareness**: Time spent in reflection, much like time spent in a burrow, allows us to develop self-awareness. This awareness is the foundation for making meaningful changes in our lives.
- **Healing and Growth**: Burrowing can also symbolize the healing process, where we retreat to address wounds, process emotions, and emerge stronger. It reminds us that rest and solitude are not weaknesses but essential components of resilience.

The psychological benefits of introspection, as symbolized by burrowing, underscore the importance of creating intentional time and space for self-reflection.

Lessons in Retreat and Renewal

The groundhog's burrowing behavior teaches us the value of retreat—not as an act of avoidance but as a necessary step toward renewal and strength. In a world that often prioritizes constant action, the groundhog reminds us of the power of stillness.

- **The Strength in Retreat**: By retreating to its burrow, the groundhog demonstrates that stepping back is not a sign of weakness but a strategy for survival and preparation. For humans, taking time to reflect allows us to recharge and approach challenges with greater clarity.
- **Creating a Personal Sanctuary**: The groundhog's burrow is carefully crafted to meet its needs. Similarly, we must create personal sanctuaries—physical or mental spaces where we can reflect, heal, and grow.
- **Embracing Solitude**: The solitude of the burrow is a reminder that being alone can be a powerful and enriching experience. It is in moments of solitude that we can connect most deeply with ourselves.

These lessons encourage us to view reflection as an essential and enriching part of life, rather than a luxury or an afterthought.

Burrowing as a Universal Metaphor

While the groundhog's burrow is unique to its species, the concept of burrowing is universal. Across cultures and traditions, the idea of retreating into a safe, hidden space for reflection and renewal appears in various forms, from meditation practices to sacred rituals.

- **Caves and Sanctuaries**: In many traditions, caves are symbolic of introspection and spiritual enlightenment. Like the groundhog's burrow, they represent spaces where transformation occurs.
- **Hibernation and Rest**: The act of hibernation is a metaphor for the cycles of life, where rest and retreat lead to growth and renewal.
- **Tunnels of Transition**: Tunnels, like burrows, symbolize journeys of transition—moving from one state of being to another. They remind us that reflection is often a precursor to change.

By viewing burrowing as a universal metaphor, we can draw inspiration from the groundhog's behavior and apply its lessons to our own lives.

Practical Applications of the Burrowing Metaphor

The metaphor of burrowing can be applied in practical ways to enhance our daily lives and personal growth:

- **Journaling**: Writing can serve as a form of burrowing, helping us delve into our thoughts and uncover insights.
- **Mindful Retreats**: Setting aside dedicated time for reflection, whether through meditation, nature walks, or solitude, mirrors the groundhog's retreat to its burrow.
- **Creating Safe Spaces**: Designing physical spaces that foster relaxation and introspection—such as a cozy reading nook or a meditation corner—can enhance our ability to reflect and recharge.

By integrating these practices into our lives, we can cultivate a deeper connection to ourselves and the rhythms of nature.

Emerging from the Burrow

The act of burrowing is not the end of the story—it is the prelude to emergence. After spending time underground, the groundhog re-emerges into the world, renewed and ready to face its challenges. This cycle of retreat and return serves as a powerful metaphor for personal growth and transformation.

As we reflect on the lessons of burrowing, we are reminded that the act of retreating inward is not a sign of retreating from life. Instead, it is an intentional pause that allows us to gather strength, gain clarity, and prepare for the journey ahead. Just as the groundhog relies on its burrow for survival, we can rely on moments of introspection to guide us toward greater understanding and fulfillment.

Chapter 4: Cycles of Hibernation and Renewal

The groundhog's annual cycle of hibernation and renewal serves as one of nature's most profound metaphors for resilience, adaptation, and the transformative power of rest. This cycle, rooted in the rhythm of the seasons, illustrates the delicate balance between conservation and action, dormancy and growth. In this chapter, we delve into the biological and symbolic significance of hibernation and renewal, exploring the lessons it offers for human life and personal development.

The Biological Miracle of Hibernation

Hibernation is a state of suspended animation, a biological adaptation that allows animals like the groundhog to survive harsh winters. During this period, the groundhog undergoes remarkable physiological changes to conserve energy and sustain life when food is scarce.

- **Metabolic Slowdown**: The groundhog's body temperature drops from around 99°F to just above freezing, and its heart rate decreases from 80 beats per minute to as low as 5 beats per minute. This extreme conservation of energy is crucial for survival.
- **Fat Reserves as Fuel**: Before hibernation, the groundhog builds up fat reserves by consuming large amounts of food in the late summer and fall. These reserves provide the energy needed to sustain the animal through months of dormancy.
- **Periodic Arousals**: Unlike some other hibernating species, groundhogs periodically awaken during hibernation to adjust their positions, relieve themselves, and maintain minimal bodily functions. These brief moments of activity ensure the groundhog's body remains functional throughout the hibernation period.

From a biological perspective, hibernation exemplifies the importance of preparation, efficiency, and adaptation in surviving challenging conditions.

The Symbolism of Hibernation

Beyond its biological function, hibernation serves as a powerful metaphor for the human experience. It represents the necessity of retreat and rest in the face of life's difficulties, as well as the potential for growth and renewal that follows periods of dormancy.

- **Rest as a Foundation for Growth**: Hibernation reminds us that rest is not a luxury but a vital part of any cycle of progress. Just as the groundhog conserves energy during the winter, humans must also take time to recharge to thrive.
- **Facing the Inner World**: The act of retreating into a burrow for hibernation mirrors the human need for introspection. It is during these quiet moments that we can confront our fears, process our emotions, and gain clarity.
- **The Promise of Renewal**: Hibernation carries the implicit promise of spring—a time of reawakening and new opportunities. This cycle of dormancy and renewal reflects the broader patterns of life, where periods of rest lead to growth and transformation.

The groundhog's hibernation teaches us to embrace stillness as an essential component of resilience and success.

Renewal: Emerging Stronger

When the groundhog emerges from its burrow in the spring, it symbolizes the culmination of the hibernation cycle: renewal. This emergence is not just a return to activity but a transformation, where the animal reclaims its energy and resumes its role in the ecosystem.

- **Physical Renewal**: The fat reserves that sustained the groundhog during hibernation are replaced by fresh food and activity, rejuvenating its body.
- **Behavioral Shifts**: With the return of spring, the groundhog transitions from a state of conservation to one of action, focusing on foraging, mating, and repairing or expanding its burrow.
- **A Return to Connection**: Emerging from hibernation also marks the groundhog's reconnection with the world above ground, a metaphor for re-engaging with community and opportunities after a period of solitude.

This process underscores the cyclical nature of life, where periods of inactivity are followed by dynamic growth and renewed purpose.

Lessons for Human Life

The groundhog's cycles of hibernation and renewal offer valuable lessons for navigating the complexities of human life. By embracing these natural rhythms, we can achieve greater balance, resilience, and fulfillment.

- **The Importance of Rest**: In a culture that often glorifies constant activity, the groundhog's hibernation reminds us that rest is essential for long-term success. Taking time to recharge allows us to avoid burnout and approach challenges with clarity and energy.
- **Preparation for Challenges**: Just as the groundhog builds up fat reserves to sustain itself during hibernation, we must prepare for difficult times by developing emotional, physical, and financial resilience.
- **Embracing Change**: The transition from hibernation to renewal illustrates the importance of adaptability. By accepting the ebb and flow of life, we can move through periods of difficulty with grace and emerge stronger.

These lessons encourage us to view rest and renewal not as opposing forces but as complementary aspects of a balanced life.

Cycles in Nature and Human Life

The groundhog's cycle of hibernation and renewal is a reflection of broader patterns in nature, where cycles govern the behavior of all living things. By observing these patterns, we can gain insights into our own lives.

- **The Seasonal Cycle**: Like the groundhog, humans are influenced by the changing seasons. Winter often brings a natural inclination to slow down and reflect, while spring inspires action and growth.
- **The Cycle of Growth**: Personal and professional growth often follows a cycle of rest, preparation, and action. Periods of dormancy, such as taking a sabbatical or pausing to reassess goals, can lead to breakthroughs and new opportunities.
- **The Cycle of Healing**: Emotional healing also follows a cyclical pattern, where time spent processing pain or loss leads to renewal and a greater sense of peace.

By aligning our lives with these natural cycles, we can cultivate resilience and adaptability, just as the groundhog does.

Practical Applications of the Hibernation Cycle

The principles of hibernation and renewal can be applied to various aspects of human life, offering practical strategies for achieving balance and growth.

- **Incorporating Rest Periods**: Schedule regular breaks or sabbaticals to recharge and reflect. Whether through vacations, meditation, or simply unplugging from technology, intentional rest can boost productivity and creativity.
- **Preparing for Challenges**: Build emotional and financial reserves to sustain yourself during difficult times. Just as the groundhog relies on fat stores, humans benefit from having resources to draw upon when needed.
- **Embracing New Beginnings**: Use the transition from rest to activity as an opportunity to set fresh goals and pursue new endeavors. Like the groundhog emerging in spring, approach each new cycle with renewed energy and purpose.

These strategies help us align our actions with nature's rhythms, fostering a more harmonious and fulfilling life.

The Eternal Cycle

The groundhog's cycle of hibernation and renewal is not a one-time event but a recurring process that repeats throughout its life. This continuity reflects the enduring nature of life's rhythms and the importance of embracing each phase with intention and awareness.

As we observe the groundhog's journey, we are reminded that life is not a linear path but a series of cycles. Each period of rest prepares us for growth, and each phase of activity leads us back to rest. By honoring these cycles, we can find balance and resilience in the face of life's challenges.

The groundhog's story is a testament to the wisdom of nature's design, offering insights that inspire us to live in harmony with the world around us and within ourselves. As we continue our exploration of the groundhog's symbolic life, let us carry these lessons forward, finding strength and renewal in the rhythms of life.

Chapter 5: Finding Your Own Seasonal Rhythm

Life, like nature, operates on cycles—periods of activity, rest, renewal, and growth. Just as the groundhog's life is governed by the seasons, humans also thrive when they align with their own natural rhythms. However, finding and honoring this personal rhythm requires introspection, mindfulness, and a willingness to adapt. In this chapter, we explore the concept of seasonal rhythms, how they manifest in human life, and practical strategies for discovering and aligning with your unique cycle.

Understanding Seasonal Rhythms

Seasonal rhythms are patterns of energy and activity that reflect the ebb and flow of time. These rhythms are influenced by nature, biology, and personal circumstances. For the groundhog, these rhythms are intuitive, tied to the changing seasons. For humans, they may be less obvious but equally vital.

- **Physical Rhythms**: Our bodies respond to natural cycles, such as the circadian rhythm (daily cycles of sleep and wakefulness) and the infradian rhythm (longer cycles, like the menstrual cycle). These rhythms influence energy levels, mood, and productivity.
- **Emotional Rhythms**: Emotions also follow patterns, often tied to external factors like weather or life events. For example, many people experience heightened energy and optimism in spring and summer, while autumn and winter may bring introspection or melancholy.
- **Cultural Rhythms**: Societal expectations and traditions, such as holidays or fiscal years, create external rhythms that influence how we structure our time and goals.

Recognizing these rhythms is the first step toward understanding how they affect your life and how you can align with them.

The Importance of Alignment

Living out of sync with your seasonal rhythm can lead to stress, burnout, and a sense of disconnection. Conversely, aligning with these rhythms allows you to flow with life's natural currents, enhancing well-being and productivity.

- **Increased Energy**: By matching your activities to your energy levels, you can maximize productivity during high-energy periods and rest effectively during low-energy times.
- **Improved Mental Health**: Seasonal alignment fosters a sense of harmony, reducing anxiety and creating space for introspection and growth.
- **Greater Resilience**: Understanding your rhythms helps you prepare for challenges and embrace opportunities with greater confidence.

Just as the groundhog prepares for winter by hibernating, you can prepare for periods of challenge or transition by attuning to your personal rhythms.

Identifying Your Seasonal Rhythm

Finding your seasonal rhythm involves observing patterns in your energy, emotions, and productivity over time. The following steps can help you uncover your natural cycle:

1. **Track Your Energy Levels**: Keep a journal for a month, noting your energy, mood, and focus throughout the day. Look for patterns—do you feel more energized in the morning, afternoon, or evening? Are there specific days or weeks when you feel particularly productive or introspective?

2. **Reflect on Seasonal Changes**: Consider how the changing seasons affect you. Do you feel more motivated in spring? Do you prefer introspection during winter? Recognizing these patterns can help you plan your activities accordingly.

3. **Listen to Your Body**: Pay attention to physical cues, such as fatigue, hunger, or restlessness. These signals often indicate where you are in your rhythm and what your body needs.

4. **Identify Emotional Patterns**: Notice how your emotions fluctuate throughout the year. Are there times when you feel more creative, social, or contemplative? Understanding these emotional cycles can guide your priorities.

5. **Consider External Influences**: Acknowledge the impact of work, family, and societal expectations on your rhythm. While you may not have complete control over these factors, recognizing their influence can help you find balance.

By combining these observations, you can begin to map out your seasonal rhythm and make intentional choices about how to structure your time.

Creating a Life Aligned with Your Rhythm

Once you understand your seasonal rhythm, the next step is to create a life that honors and supports it. This involves setting realistic goals, adjusting your schedule, and building habits that align with your natural cycles.

- **Set Seasonal Goals**: Break your year into seasons and set goals that align with each phase. For example:
    - **Spring**: Focus on new beginnings, such as starting a project or learning a new skill.
    - **Summer**: Embrace growth and activity by tackling ambitious goals or expanding your social circle.
    - **Autumn**: Shift toward reflection and preparation, evaluating your progress and setting intentions for the future.
    - **Winter**: Prioritize rest, introspection, and planning, allowing yourself to recharge.
- **Structure Your Days and Weeks**: Design your daily and weekly schedules to reflect your energy patterns. Plan high-energy tasks for your most productive times and reserve low-energy periods for rest or routine activities.
- **Build Rest into Your Routine**: Like the groundhog's hibernation, rest is an essential part of your rhythm. Schedule regular breaks, practice mindfulness, and create a bedtime routine that supports restorative sleep.
- **Adapt to Life's Changes**: Remember that your rhythm may shift over time due to changes in health, circumstances, or environment. Stay flexible and adjust your approach as needed.

Overcoming Challenges to Alignment

Aligning with your seasonal rhythm is not always easy. Modern life often demands constant activity, leaving little room for rest or reflection. However, with intention and effort, you can navigate these challenges.

- **Challenge: Overcommitment**
  - **Solution**: Learn to say no and prioritize activities that align with your rhythm. Use tools like time-blocking to protect periods of rest and focus.
- **Challenge: Societal Expectations**
  - **Solution**: Advocate for your needs and educate others about the importance of seasonal rhythms. For example, explain to colleagues why you prefer morning meetings or why you take breaks during the day.
- **Challenge: Unexpected Events**
  - **Solution**: Build flexibility into your schedule to accommodate disruptions. Recognize that periods of misalignment are temporary and focus on returning to your rhythm when possible.

By addressing these challenges, you can create a sustainable lifestyle that honors your natural cycles.

Lessons from the Groundhog

The groundhog's seasonal rhythm offers timeless lessons for humans seeking balance and harmony in their lives:

1. **Prepare for Each Season**: Just as the groundhog builds fat reserves for winter, prepare for transitions by setting aside resources, building skills, and fostering resilience.
2. **Honor Rest and Renewal**: Hibernation is not a weakness but a survival strategy. Embrace rest as an essential part of your rhythm, allowing yourself time to recharge.
3. **Embrace Change**: Seasons change, and so do we. Adapt to life's shifts with flexibility and curiosity, viewing each phase as an opportunity for growth.
4. **Stay Connected to Nature**: Like the groundhog, you are part of the natural world. Spending time in nature can help you reconnect with its rhythms and find inspiration for your own journey.

Practical Exercises for Tuning into Your Rhythm

To deepen your connection with your seasonal rhythm, try the following exercises:

1. **Seasonal Reflection**: At the start of each season, reflect on your goals, energy levels, and priorities. Write down what you hope to achieve and how you plan to align with the season's energy.
2. **Energy Mapping**: Create a visual map of your daily and weekly energy patterns. Use this map to plan your schedule and identify periods for rest and focus.
3. **Nature Connection**: Spend time outdoors each week, observing how the environment changes with the seasons. Use these observations to inspire your own cycles of growth and renewal.
4. **Mindful Journaling**: Write daily or weekly journal entries about your thoughts, emotions, and experiences. Over time, look for patterns that reveal your rhythm.

Conclusion

Finding your seasonal rhythm is a journey of self-discovery and adaptation. By observing your energy patterns, aligning with nature's cycles, and creating intentional habits, you can live a more balanced and fulfilling life. Like the groundhog, you have the power to prepare for challenges, embrace rest, and emerge renewed with each passing season.

As you continue to explore your rhythm, remember that alignment is not about perfection but about awareness and intention. The more you honor your natural cycles, the more you will thrive—just as the groundhog thrives by living in harmony with the rhythms of the earth.

Appendix A: Self-Reflection Prompts Inspired by the Groundhog

The groundhog's behavior—its retreat into the burrow, cycles of hibernation, and eventual reemergence—provides a wealth of metaphors for self-reflection and personal growth. Inspired by these behaviors, the following prompts are designed to help you delve into your inner world, gain clarity, and align with the natural rhythms of your life. These prompts are grouped by themes derived from the groundhog's symbolic life: introspection, preparation, renewal, and connection with nature.

Section 1: Introspection – Exploring Your Inner Burrow

The groundhog retreats into its burrow for safety, rest, and reflection. Use these prompts to explore your own inner sanctuary and uncover hidden truths.

1. **Your Safe Haven**
   ◦ What does your ideal "burrow" look like—physically, emotionally, or spiritually?
   ◦ Where do you feel safest and most at peace? How can you create more spaces like this in your life?
2. **Confronting Shadows**
   ◦ What fears or insecurities have you been avoiding?
   ◦ How can you begin to face these challenges with courage and self-compassion?
3. **Your Inner Resources**
   ◦ What strengths or talents lie dormant within you?
   ◦ How can you nurture and bring these strengths to the surface?

4. Hidden Chambers

- If your mind were a burrow with different chambers, what would each chamber represent?
- Which chamber feels most neglected, and how can you bring attention to it?

Section 2: Preparation – Building Your Foundation

The groundhog meticulously prepares for winter, storing resources and creating a secure burrow. Reflect on how you prepare for challenges and future opportunities.

1. Planning for the Future

- What steps are you taking to prepare for your goals?
- Are there areas where you feel unprepared? How can you address these gaps?

2. Resource Gathering

- What emotional, physical, or financial resources do you need to feel secure?
- How can you begin to build these reserves?

3. Habits of Success

- What daily or weekly habits contribute to your long-term well-being?
- Are there habits you need to let go of to make room for more productive ones?

4. Adaptability

- How do you respond when your plans are disrupted?
- What can you do to become more flexible and resilient in the face of change?

Section 3: Renewal – Emerging Stronger

The groundhog emerges from hibernation renewed and ready to face the challenges of spring. These prompts help you explore your own cycles of rest and renewal.

1. **The Importance of Rest**
    - When was the last time you truly rested, both physically and mentally?
    - What prevents you from taking time to recharge, and how can you overcome these barriers?
2. **Signs of Renewal**
    - What signs in your life indicate that it's time for a fresh start?
    - How can you embrace renewal without fear or hesitation?
3. **Lessons from Dormancy**
    - Think of a time when you felt "dormant" or stuck. What did you learn from that period?
    - How did that experience prepare you for the next phase of growth?
4. **Emerging with Purpose**
    - What new opportunities or challenges are you preparing to face?
    - How can you emerge from your "burrow" with confidence and intention?

Section 4: Connection with Nature – Aligning with Cycles

The groundhog's life is in harmony with the rhythms of nature. Use these prompts to reflect on your connection to the natural world and its influence on your personal rhythms.

1. **Seasonal Patterns**
   - How do the changing seasons affect your energy, mood, and productivity?
   - What rituals or practices help you stay connected to the seasons?

2. **Nature's Lessons**
   - What lessons have you learned from observing the natural world?
   - How can you incorporate these lessons into your daily life?

3. **Finding Your Rhythm**
   - What does your personal rhythm look like—daily, weekly, or yearly?
   - How can you align your actions and goals with this rhythm?

4. **Moments of Stillness**
   - When was the last time you spent quiet, intentional time in nature?
   - How can you create more opportunities to experience stillness and connection with the earth?

Section 5: Personal Transformation – Embracing Change

The groundhog's cyclical journey is a metaphor for transformation and growth. Reflect on how you navigate change and embrace new opportunities.

1. **Letting Go**
   - What are you holding onto that no longer serves you?
   - How can you let go to make space for growth and renewal?

2. **Embracing Change**
   - What changes in your life have been the most transformative?
   - How did you grow from these experiences, and what did you learn about yourself?

3. **A Vision for the Future**
   - What does your ideal future look like?
   - What steps can you take now to bring that vision closer to reality?

4. **Reinvention**
   - If you could reinvent one aspect of your life, what would it be?
   - What actions can you take to begin this transformation?

Section 6: Gratitude and Reflection – Celebrating Growth

The groundhog's life is a reminder of the beauty of cycles and the importance of gratitude. Use these prompts to celebrate your progress and express appreciation for the journey.

1. **Recognizing Growth**
   - What progress have you made over the past year?
   - How can you honor and celebrate your accomplishments?
2. **Gratitude for Challenges**
   - What challenges have shaped you into the person you are today?
   - How can you express gratitude for the lessons they've taught you?
3. **Appreciating the Journey**
   - How has your journey—through rest, reflection, and renewal—shaped your perspective on life?
   - What steps can you take to continue growing while staying true to yourself?
4. **Giving Back**
   - How can you share the wisdom you've gained with others?
   - In what ways can you support or inspire those around you to embrace their own rhythms?

Conclusion

The groundhog's life offers profound insights into the power of introspection, preparation, and renewal. These self-reflection prompts invite you to explore your own journey, aligning with the rhythms of nature and your unique cycles of growth. By engaging with these questions, you can uncover hidden truths, embrace change, and live a more intentional and fulfilling life. Let the lessons of the groundhog guide you as you burrow deep into your soul, emerge with clarity, and thrive with renewed purpose.

Message from the Author:

I hope you enjoyed this book, I love astrology and knew there was not a book such as this out on the shelf. I love metaphysical items as well. Please check out my other books:

-Life of Government Benefits

-My life of Hell

-My life with Hydrocephalus

-Red Sky

-World Domination:Woman's rule

-World Domination:Woman's Rule 2: The War

-Life and Banishment of Apophis: book 1

-The Kidney Friendly Diet

-The Ultimate Hemp Cookbook

-Creating a Dispensary(legally)

-Cleanliness throughout life: the importance of showering from childhood to adulthood.

-Strong Roots: The Risks of Overcoddling children

-Hemp Horoscopes: Cosmic Insights and Earthly Healing

- Celestial Hemp Navigating the Zodiac: Through the Green Cosmos

-Astrological Hemp: Aligning The Stars with Earth's Ancient Herb

-The Astrological Guide to Hemp: Stars, Signs, and Sacred Leaves

-Green Growth: Innovative Marketing Strategies for your Hemp Products and Dispensary

-Cosmic Cannabis

-Astrological Munchies

-Henry The Hemp

-Zodiacal Roots: The Astrological Soul Of Hemp

- **Green Constellations: Intersection of Hemp and Zodiac**

-Hemp in The Houses: An astrological Adventure Through The Cannabis Galaxy

-Galactic Ganja Guide

Heavenly Hemp

Zodiac Leaves

Doctor Who Astrology

Cannastrology

Stellar Satvias and Cosmic Indicas

<u>Celestial Cannabis: A Zodiac Journey</u>

AstroHerbology: The Sky and The Soil: Volume 1

AstroHerbology:Celestial Cannabis:Volume 2

Cosmic Cannabis Cultivation

The Starry Guide to Herbal Harmony: Volume 1

The Starry Guide to Herbal Harmony: Cannabis Universe: Volume 2

Yugioh Astrology: Astrological Guide to Deck, Duels and more

Nightmare Mansion: Echoes of The Abyss

Nightmare Mansion 2: Legacy of Shadows

Nightmare Mansion 3: Shadows of the Forgotten

Nightmare Mansion 4: Echoes of the Damned

The Life and Banishment of Apophis: Book 2

Nightmare Mansion: Halls of Despair

<u>Healing with Herb: Cannabis and Hydrocephalus</u>

<u>Planetary Pot: Aligning with Astrological Herbs: Volume 1</u>

Fast Track to Freedom: 30 Days to Financial Independence Using AI, Assets, and Agile Hustles

<u>Cosmic Hemp Pathways</u>

How to Become Financially Free in 30 Days: 10,000 Paths to Prosperity

Zodiacal Herbage: Astrological Insights: Volume 1

Nightmare Mansion: Whispers in the Walls

The Daleks Invade Atlantis

Henry the hemp and Hydrocephalus

10X The Kidney Friendly Diet

Cannabis Universe: Adult coloring book

Hemp Astrology: The Healing Power of the Stars

Zodiacal Herbage: Astrological Insights: Cannabis Universe: Volume 2

<u>Planetary Pot: Aligning with Astrological Herbs: Cannabis Universes: Volume 2</u>

Doctor Who Meets the Replicators and SG-1: The Ultimate Battle for Survival

Nightmare Mansion: Curse of the Blood Moon

<u>The Celestial Stoner: A Guide to the Zodiac</u>

Cosmic Pleasures: Sex Toy Astrology for Every Sign

Hydrocephalus Astrology: Navigating the Stars and Healing Waters

Lapis and the Mischievous Chocolate Bar

Celestial Positions: Sexual Astrology for Every Sign

Apophis's Shadow Work Journal: : A Journey of Self-Discovery and Healing

Kinky Cosmos: Sexual Kink Astrology for Every Sign

Digital Cosmos: The Astrological Digimon Compendium

Stellar Seeds: The Cosmic Guide to Growing with Astrology

Apophis's Daily Gratitude Journal

Cat Astrology: Feline Mysteries of the Cosmos

The Cosmic Kama Sutra: An Astrological Guide to Sexual Positions

Unleash Your Potential: A Guided Journal Powered by AI Insights

Whispers of the Enchanted Grove

Cosmic Pleasures: An Astrological Guide to Sexual Kinks

369, 12 Manifestation Journal

Whisper of the nocturne journal(blank journal for writing or drawing)

The Boogey Book

Locked In Reflection: A Chastity Journey Through Locktober

Generating Wealth Quickly:

How to Generate $100,000 in 24 Hours

Star Magic: Harness the Power of the Universe

The Flatulence Chronicles: A Fart Journal for Self-Discovery

The Doctor and The Death Moth

Seize the Day: A Personal Seizure Tracking Journal

The Ultimate Boogeyman Safari: A Journey into the Boogie World and Beyond

Whispers of Samhain: 1,000 Spells of Love, Luck, and Lunar Magic: Samhain Spell Book

Apophis's guides:

Witch's Spellbook Crafting Guide for Halloween

<u>Frost & Flame: The Enchanted Yule Grimoire of 1000 Winter Spells</u>

<u>The Ultimate Boogey Goo Guide & Spooky Activities for Halloween Fun</u>

Harmony of the Scales: A Libra's Spellcraft for Balance and Beauty

The Enchanted Advent: 36 Days of Christmas Wonders

Nightmare Mansion: The Labyrinth of Screams

Harvest of Enchantment: 1,000 Spells of Gratitude, Love, and Fortune for Thanksgiving

The Boogey Chronicles: A Journal of Nightly Encounters and Shadowy Secrets

The 12 Days of Financial Freedom: A Step-by-Step Christmas Countdown to Transform Your Finances

Sigil of the Eternal Spiral Blank Journal

A Christmas Feast: Timeless Recipes for Every Meal

Holiday Stress-Free Solutions: A Survival Guide to Thriving During the Festive Season

Yu-Gi-Oh! Holiday Gifting Mastery: The Ultimate Guide for Fans and Newcomers Alike

Holiday Harmony: A Hydrocephalus Survival Guide for the Festive Season

Celestial Craft: The Witch's Almanac for 2025 – A Cosmic Guide to Manifestations, Moons, and Mystical Events

Doctor Who: The Toymaker's Winter Wonderland

Tulsa King Unveiled: A Thrilling Guide to Stallone's Mafia Masterpiece

Pendulum Craft: A Complete Guide to Crafting and Using Personalized Divination Tools

Nightmare Mansion: Santa's Eternal Eve

Starlight Noel: A Cosmic Journey through Christmas Mysteries

The Dark Architect: Unlocking the Blueprint of Existence

Surviving the Embrace: The Ultimate Guide to Encounters with The Hugging Molly

The Enchanted Codex: Secrets of the Craft for Witches, Wiccans, and Pagans

Harvest of Gratitude: A Complete Thanksgiving Guide

Yuletide Essentials: A Complete Guide to an Authentic and Magical Christmas

Celestial Smokes: A Cosmic Guide to Cigars and Astrology

Living in Balance: A Comprehensive Survival Guide to Thriving with Diabetes Insipidus

Cosmic Symbiosis: The Venom Zodiac Chronicles

The Cursed Paw of Ambition

Cosmic Symbiosis: The Astrological Venom Journal

Celestial Wonders Unfold: A Stargazer's Guide to the Cosmos (2024-2029)

The Ultimate Black Friday Prepper's Guide: Mastering Shopping Strategies and Savings

Cosmic Sales: The Astrological Guide to Black Friday Shopping
Legends of the Corn Mother and Other Harvest Myths
Whispers of the Harvest: The Corn Mother's Journal
The Evergreen Spellbook
The Doctor Meets the Boogeyman
The White Witch of Rose Hall's SpellBook
The Gingerbread Golem's Shadow: A Study in Sweet Darkness
The Gingerbread Golem Codex: An Academic Exploration of Sweet Myths
The Gingerbread Golem Grimoire: Sweet Magicks and Spells for the Festive Witch
The Curse of the Gingerbread Golem
10-minute Christmas Crafts for kids
<u>Christmas Crisis Solutions: The Ultimate Last-Minute Survival Guide</u>
Gingerbread Golem Recipes: Holiday Treats with a Magical Twist
The Infinite Key: Unlocking Mystical Secrets of the Ages
Enchanted Yule: A Wiccan and Pagan Guide to a Magical and Memorable Season
Dinosaurs of Power: Unlocking Ancient Magick
Astro-Dinos: The Cosmic Guide to Prehistoric Wisdom
Gallifrey's Yule Logs: A Festive Doctor Who Cookbook
The Dino Grimoire: Secrets of Prehistoric Magick
The Gift They Never Knew They Needed
The Gingerbread Golem's Culinary Alchemy: Enchanting Recipes for a Sweetly Dark Feast
A Time Lord Christmas: Holiday Adventures with the Doctor
Krampusproofing Your Home: Defensive Strategies for Yule
Silent Frights: A Collection of Christmas Creepypastas to Chill Your Bones
Santa Raptor's Jolly Carnage: A Dino-Claus Christmas Tale
Prehistoric Palettes: A Dino Wicca Coloring Journey
The Christmas Wishkeeper Chronicles

The Starlight Sleigh: A Holiday Journey

Elf Secrets: The True Magic of the North Pole

Candy Cane Conjurations

Cooking with Kids: Recipes Under 20 Minutes

Doctor Who: The TARDIS Confiscation

The Anxiety First Aid Kit: Quick Tools to Calm Your Mind

Frosty Whispers: A Winter's Tale

The Infinite Key: Unlocking the Secrets to Prosperity, Resilience, and Purpose

The Grasping Void: Why You'll Regret This Purchase

Astrology for Busy Bees: Star Signs Simplified

The Instant Focus Formula: Cut Through the Noise

The Secret Language of Colors: Unlocking the Emotional Codes

Sacred Fossil Chronicles: Blank Journal

The Christmas Cottage Miracle

Feeding Frenzy: Graboid-Inspired Recipes

Manifest in Minutes: The Quick Law of Attraction Guide

The Symbiote Chronicles: Doctor Who's Venomous Journey

Think Tiny, Grow Big: The Minimalist Mindset

The Energy Key: Unlocking Limitless Motivation

New Year, New Magic: Manifesting Your Best Year Yet

Unstoppable You: Mastering Confidence in Minutes

Infinite Energy: The Secret to Never Feeling Drained

Lightning Focus: Mastering the Art of Productivity in a Distracted World

Saturnalia Manifestation Magick: A Guide to Unlocking Abundance During the Solstice

Graboids and Garland: The Ultimate Tremors-Themed Christmas Guide

12 Nights of Holiday Magic

The Power of Pause: 60-Second Mindfulness Practices

The Quick Reset: How to Reclaim Your Life After Burnout

The Shadow Eater: A Tale of Despair and Survival

The Micro-Mastery Method: Transform Your Skills in Just Minutes a Day

Reclaiming Time: How to Live More by Doing Less

Chronovore: The Eternal Nexus

The Mind Reset: Unlocking Your Inner Peace in a Chaotic World

Confidence Code: Building Unshakable Self-Belief

Baby the Vampire Terrier

Baby the Vampire Terrier's Christmas Adventure

Celestial Streams: The Content Creator's Astrology Manual

The Wealth Whisperer: Unlocking Abundance with Everyday Actions

The Energy Equation: Maximize Your Output Without Burning Out

The Happiness Algorithm: Science-Backed Steps to Joyful Living

Stress-Free Success: Achieving Goals Without Anxiety

Mindful Wealth: The New Blueprint for Financial Freedom

The Festive Flavors of New Year: A Culinary Celebration

The Master's Gambit: Keys of Eternal Power

Shadowed Secrets: Groundhog Day Mysteries

If you want solar for your home go here: https://www.harborso-
lar.live/apophisenterprises/

Get Some Tarot cards: https://www.makeplayingcards.com/sell/
apophis-occult-shop

Get some   shirts: https://www.bonfire.com/store/apophis-shirt-emporium/

Instagrams:
@apophis_enterprises,
@apophisbookemporium,
@apophisscardshop
Twitter: @apophisenterpr1
Tiktok:@apophisenterprise
Youtube: @sg1fan23477, @FiresideRetreatKingdom
Hive: @sg1fan23477
CheeLee: @SG1fan23477

Podcast: Apophis Chat Zone: https://open.spotify.com/show/
5zXbrCLEV2xzCp8ybrfHsk?si=fb4d4fdbdce44dec

Newsletter: https://apophiss-newsletter-27c897.beehiiv.com/

If you want to support me or see posts of other projects that I have come over to: **buymeacoffee.com/mpetchinskg**
I post there daily several times a day

Get your Dinowicca or Christmas themed digital products, especially Santa Raptor songs and other musics. Here:
https://sg1fan23477.gumroad.com

Apophis Yuletide Digital has not only digital Christmas items, but it will have all things with Dinowicca as well as other Digital products.